Our Favorite Apple recipes

Copyright 2023, Gooseberry Patch
Previously published under ISBN 978-1-62093-282-7
Cover: French Apple Crisp (page 119)

Pile shiny red apples in a rustic wooden bowl
for a welcoming centerpiece.

Apple Breakfast Cobbler

4 apples, peeled, cored and sliced
1/4 c. honey
1 t. cinnamon

2 T. butter, melted
2 c. granola cereal
Garnish: milk or cream

Place apples in a slow cooker sprayed with non-stick vegetable spray.
In a bowl, combine remaining ingredients except garnish; sprinkle over
apples. Cover and cook on low setting for 7 to 9 hours, or on high setting
for 3 to 4 hours. Garnish with milk or cream.

Planning a midday brunch? Alongside breakfast foods like baked eggs, coffee cake and muffins, offer a light, savory main dish or two for those who have already enjoyed breakfast.

Slow-Cooker Apple Oats

Makes 6 servings

2 apples, peeled if desired,
cored and chopped
2 c. milk
1-1/2 c. water
1/4 c. brown sugar, packed

1/2 c. unsweetened applesauce
1 c. steel-cut oats, uncooked
1 T. butter
1 t. cinnamon
1/4 t. salt

Spray a 6-quart slow cooker with non-stick vegetable spray, if desired. Combine all ingredients in slow cooker; stir to combine. Cover and cook on low setting for 7 hours. Stir again before serving.

Take your family's breakfast outdoors! Spread a quilt
on the picnic table and enjoy the cool morning air.

Apple Walnut Breakfast Cake

Serves 16

3 eggs, beaten
1 c. oil
2 c. sugar
1 T. vanilla extract
3 c. all-purpose flour
1 t. salt
1/2 t. baking powder

1 t. baking soda
3/4 t. nutmeg
1 T. cinnamon
2 c. apples, peeled, cored
   and chopped
1 c. chopped walnuts

In a bowl, combine all ingredients except apples and nuts; mix well. Stir in apples and nuts; pour into greased and floured Bundt® pan. Bake at 300 degrees for 45 minutes. Increase heat to 325 degrees and bake an additional 20 minutes. Cool on a wire rack for 20 minutes; turn out onto a serving plate. Top with Glaze before serving.

Glaze:

1 c. powdered sugar
1-1/2 T. milk

1/2 t. vanilla extract

In a bowl, whisk together all ingredients.

Mismatched glass salt & pepper shakers make sweet mini vases for the breakfast table. Simply remove the tops, fill with water and tuck in a big blossom. Place one at each table setting for a colorful accent.

Autumn Amish Baked Oatmeal

Serves 6

Optional: 1/2 c. diced apples,
  1/2 c. raisins
1-1/2 c. long-cooking oats,
  uncooked
1/2 c. brown sugar, packed
1 egg, beaten

1/4 c. oil
1 c. milk
1 t. baking powder
1 t. cinnamon
Garnish: additional milk

Layer apples and/or raisins in the bottom of a greased 9"x9" baking pan, if using; set aside. Beat together remaining ingredients except garnish with a spoon. Pour oat mixture into pan. Bake, uncovered, at 300 degrees for 30 to 35 minutes. Serve topped with milk.

French toast can be frozen, how handy! Make French toast the usual way and cool completely. Layer slices with wax paper and place in a plastic freezer bag. To serve, simply pop a slice in the toaster until crisp.

Toffee Apple French Toast

Makes 8 servings

8 c. French bread, sliced into
    1-inch cubes and divided
2 Granny Smith apples, peeled,
    cored and chopped
8-oz. pkg. cream cheese, softened
3/4 c. brown sugar, packed

1/4 c. sugar
1-3/4 c. milk, divided
2 t. vanilla extract, divided
1/2 c. toffee or almond brickle
    baking bits
5 eggs, beaten

Place half the bread cubes in a greased 13"x9" baking pan; top with apples and set aside. In a medium bowl, beat cream cheese, sugars, 1/4 cup milk and one teaspoon vanilla until smooth. Stir in baking bits and spread over apples. Top with remaining bread cubes. In a separate bowl, beat eggs with remaining milk and vanilla; pour over bread. Cover and refrigerate for 8 hours to overnight. Remove from refrigerator 30 minutes before baking. Uncover and bake at 350 degrees for 35 to 45 minutes, until a knife inserted near the center comes out clean.

Stir up a super-simple fruit topping for pancakes and waffles.
Combine a can of fruit pie filling and 2 tablespoons orange juice
in a small bowl. Microwave for 2 to 2-1/2 minutes,
stirring twice. Serve warm.

Spiced Harvest Pancakes

Makes about one dozen

2-1/2 c. biscuit baking mix
1 c. milk
1 c. apple butter
2 eggs, beaten

2 T. oil
1/2 t. ground ginger
1/2 t. cinnamon
1/2 t. nutmeg

Stir together all ingredients until well blended. Pour about 1/4 cup of batter per pancake onto a hot griddle that has been sprayed with non-stick vegetable spray. Cook over medium heat until pancakes start to bubble; flip and cook until golden.

An oilcloth tablecloth with brightly colored fruit and flowers
is oh-so cheerful at breakfast…and sticky syrup and
jam spills are easily wiped off with a damp sponge!

Apple-Sausage Breakfast Ring

Serves 8

2 lbs. ground pork breakfast
    sausage
2 eggs, beaten
1-1/2 c. round buttery crackers,
    crushed

1 c. apples, peeled, cored
    and grated
1/4 c. milk

Line a Bundt® pan with plastic wrap. Combine all ingredients, mixing
well; press firmly into pan. Chill several hours or overnight. Unmold
onto an ungreased 15"x10" jelly-roll pan; remove plastic wrap. Bake at
350 degrees for one hour.

Plant the seeds of friendship and tend them
with love, patience and kindness.

–Unknown

Caramel-Apple Dip

Makes 2 cups

8-oz. pkg. cream cheese, softened
1/4 c. honey
1/2 c. caramel ice cream topping

1/4 t. cinnamon
3 to 4 Granny Smith apples,
    cored and sliced

In a serving bowl, combine cream cheese, honey, caramel topping and cinnamon; beat until smooth. Store in refrigerator until chilled. Serve with apple slices.

A new way to serve your favorite dip! Just spread
dip onto flour tortillas, roll up jelly-roll style and
cut into one-inch slices.

Sweet Apple Nachos

Makes 4 servings

3 to 4 Honey Crisp apples,
    cored and thinly sliced
1 t. lemon juice
3 T. creamy natural peanut butter
1/4 c. sliced almonds

1/4 c. chopped pecans
1/4 c. unsweetened flaked
    coconut
1/4 c. mini semi-sweet chocolate
    chips, or more to taste

Lightly coat apple slices with lemon juice to keep them from browning too fast. Arrange apples on a serving platter; set aside. Place peanut butter in a microwave-safe cup. Microwave for a short time, until very runny; drizzle 2/3 of peanut butter all over apples. Top with nuts, coconut and chocolate chips. Drizzle with remaining peanut butter. Serve immediately.

A fun icebreaker for a large gathering of all ages! Divide
into two teams...the goal is to line up alphabetically by
everyone's first names. After 60 seconds, blow a whistle
and have each team sound off by name. The team with
the most participants in alphabetical order wins!

Fruit Salsa Spread & Dip

Makes 8 servings

2 Granny Smith apples, peeled, cored and chopped
1 kiwi, peeled and chopped
1 c. strawberries, hulled and sliced, thawed if frozen
2 T. brown sugar, packed
2 T. apple jelly
juice of 1 orange
cinnamon graham crackers or vanilla wafers

In a serving bowl, combine fruit, brown sugar, jelly and juice. Mix together gently. Serve with graham crackers or vanilla wafers.

Pick up a dozen pint-size Mason jars for entertaining...
they're fun and practical for serving chilled apple cider
at an autumn get-together.

Apple-Pecan Log

8-oz. pkg. cream cheese, softened
1/2 c. tart apple, peeled, cored
  and finely chopped
3/4 c. chopped pecans, toasted
  and divided

1/4 t. cinnamon
tortilla chips, snack crackers,
  pretzels, butter cookies,
  apple slices

Combine cream cheese, apple, 1/4 cup pecans and cinnamon; mix well and form into a log. Roll log in remaining pecans. Cover with plastic wrap and chill for 3 to 5 hours, or overnight. Let stand at room temperature for 20 minutes before serving. Serve with a variety of dippers.

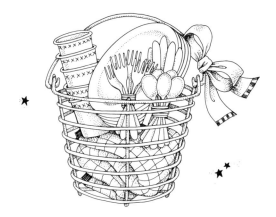

Tin pails or egg baskets are perfect for toting goodies
to and from a tailgating party. They're roomy enough
to hold paper plates, cups, napkins and a tablecloth.

24

Harvest Apple Cheese Ball

Makes 10 servings

8-oz. pkg. cream cheese, softened
1 c. shredded Cheddar cheese
1/4 t. cinnamon
3/4 c. dried apples, finely chopped
1/3 c. chopped nuts

Garnish: 2-inch cinnamon stick,
    bay leaf
assorted crackers

In a large bowl, beat cream cheese, Cheddar cheese and cinnamon until blended. Stir in dried apples. Form mixture into an apple shape; roll in chopped nuts. Insert cinnamon stick and bay leaf on top to resemble an apple's stem and leaf. Cover and refrigerate until firm. Serve with crackers.

Autumn is the perfect time of year to hit all the best craft shows, flea markets and tag sales. Call your best girlfriends, pack a basket of snacks and a thermos of spiced cider, and head out for a day of shopping fun.

Championship Meatballs

1 lb. ground pork sausage   1-1/2 T. maple syrup
1/2 c. apple butter

Form sausage into one-inch balls; place on a microwave-safe plate. Cover and microwave on high setting for one to 2 minutes, until a meat thermometer inserted in center reads 160 degrees; drain. Cool; place in a plastic zipping bag. Combine apple butter and syrup; pour over meatballs. Refrigerate overnight. Shortly before serving, transfer meatballs and sauce to a microwave-safe serving dish. Cover and microwave on high for one minute, or until heated through. Serve immediately.

Add a bit of sparkle and spice to holiday drinks...
tie a little ornament or bauble onto a cinnamon stick.
The cinnamon stick is a great stirrer, while the ornament
dangles over your mug of hot cocoa or mulled cider.

Hot Caramel Apple Cider

Serves 12

3 qts. apple cider or apple juice
6 4-inch cinnamon sticks
1/2 c. caramel ice cream topping

Garnish: whipped cream,
    additional caramel topping

Pour apple juice or cider into a slow cooker; add cinnamon sticks. Cover and cook on high setting for about 4 hours. Cinnamon sticks will soften and uncurl. Just before serving, stir in caramel topping. Serve in mugs, topped with a dollop of whipped cream and a drizzle of caramel topping.

Before the first frost, save garden cuttings to brighten
a sunny windowsill. Clip stems of impatiens or coleus, pull off
most of the leaves and slip them into water-filled Mason jars.
When roots form, plant the cuttings in potting soil and
grow indoors until spring returns.

Cranberry-Cider Spiced Tea

Makes 8 servings

8 orange spice teabags
4 c. boiling water
2 c. unsweetened cranberry juice
2 c. apple cider
1/2 c. brown sugar, packed

4-inch cinnamon stick
4 whole cloves
1/2 t. ground ginger
Garnish: orange slices

In a large saucepan, place teabags in boiling water; steep for 3 to 5 minutes. Discard teabags; add cranberry juice, cider, brown sugar and spices. Heat almost to boiling, stir until sugar dissolves. Strain to remove whole spices. Pour into teacups; garnish with orange slices.

Stir caramel topping into a mug of hot cider
for an instant warmer-upper.

Apple Cider Punch

6 c. apple cider
2 c. cranberry-raspberry
    juice cocktail
1/2 c. lemon juice

25.4-oz. bottle sparkling white
    grape juice, chilled
Optional: 1 apple, thinly sliced

Combine cider, cranberry-raspberry juice and lemon juice in a large
pitcher or punch bowl. Slowly add sparkling juice; serve immediately.
If desired, garnish glasses with apple slices.

A great way to keep brown sugar from hardening
is to drop a slice of fresh apple in the bag...
it absorbs extra moisture.

Apple-Cheddar Bread

Makes 2 loaves

3 c. all-purpose flour
2 T. baking powder
3/4 t. salt
1/2 c. sugar
1-1/2 c. milk
1/2 c. oil

1 egg, beaten
1 egg yolk, beaten
1 apple, peeled, cored and diced
1 c. shredded sharp Cheddar
    cheese

Combine flour, baking powder, salt and sugar in a large bowl; mix well and set aside. Combine milk, oil, whole egg and egg yolk in a separate bowl; add to flour mixture, stirring just until moistened. Gently fold in apple and cheese. Divide batter between 2 greased 8"x4" loaf pans. Bake at 350 degrees for about 40 minutes, until a toothpick inserted in center comes out clean. Cool in pans on a wire rack for 10 minutes. Remove from pans and cool completely on a wire rack. Store in the refrigerator.

A large square napkin or a pretty linen kitchen towel
will make a cozy liner for a basket of warm muffins.

Sweet Apple Butter Muffins

Makes one dozen

1-3/4 c. all-purpose flour
1/3 c. plus 2 T. sugar, divided
2 t. baking powder
1/2 t. cinnamon
1/4 t. nutmeg
1/4 t. salt

1 egg, beaten
3/4 c. milk
1/4 c. oil
1 t. vanilla extract
1/3 c. apple butter
1/3 c. chopped pecans

Combine flour, 1/3 cup sugar, baking powder, spices and salt in a large bowl; set aside. In a separate bowl, blend egg, milk, oil and vanilla together; stir into flour mixture. Spoon one tablespoon batter into each of 12 paper-lined muffin cups; top with one teaspoon apple butter. Fill muffin cups 2/3 full using remaining batter; set aside. Toss pecans with remaining sugar; sprinkle evenly over muffins. Bake at 400 degrees for about 20 minutes, until a toothpick inserted in the center tests clean.

The flavor of bread shared has no equal.

– Antoine de Saint-Exupery

Farmhouse Apple Bread

Makes 2 loaves

3 eggs, beaten
2 c. sugar
1 c. oil
1 T. vanilla extract
3 c. all-purpose flour

1 t. baking soda
1 t. cinnamon
3 to 4 apples, peeled, cored
   and chopped
1 c. chopped pecans

Combine eggs, sugar, oil and vanilla until well mixed; set aside. Combine flour, baking soda and cinnamon in a separate bowl; stir into egg mixture. Fold in apples and pecans. Divide equally between 2 greased and floured 9"x5" loaf pans. Bake at 325 degrees for one hour and 10 minutes.

If a muffin recipe doesn't fill all the cups in your
muffin tin, add some water to the empty cups.
This allows the muffins to bake more evenly.

Cinnamon Apple-Raisin Muffins *Makes one dozen*

1 c. all-purpose flour
1 c. whole-wheat flour
3/4 t. baking soda
1/2 t. salt
1 t. cinnamon
3/4 c. unsweetened applesauce
1/4 c. oil
1 c. sugar

1 egg, beaten
1/4 c. egg white substitute
1 t. vanilla extract
2 c. apples, peeled, cored
   and diced
1 c. raisins
1/2 c. chopped walnuts

In a bowl, stir together flours, baking soda, salt and cinnamon; set aside.
In a separate large bowl, beat applesauce, oil and sugar with an electric
mixer on low speed for 2 minutes. Add egg, egg white substitute and
vanilla; beat for one minute and set aside. Add flour mixture to applesauce
mixture; stir just until moistened. Fold in remaining ingredients. Spoon
batter into 12 paper-lined muffin cups, filling 2/3 full. Bake at 400 degrees
for 25 to 30 minutes, until a toothpick inserted in center tests clean.
Remove muffins from tin to a wire rack; serve warm or cooled.

Need a little snack while the soup is simmering? Slice up some fresh veggies and serve with this super-simple dip. Blend one cup sour cream or Greek yogurt, one cup cottage cheese, one finely sliced green onion and one packet dried vegetable soup mix.

Chicken & Apple Wild Rice Soup

Serves 8 to 10

2 T. olive oil
2 carrots, peeled and chopped
1 onion, chopped
3 stalks celery, chopped
4 qts. chicken broth
4 boneless, skinless chicken
    breasts, cooked and shredded

1/3 c. wild rice, uncooked
2 t. dried tarragon
1 T. fresh parsley, chopped
salt and pepper to taste
3 Granny Smith apples, peeled,
    cored and chopped

Heat oil in a stockpot over medium heat. Sauté vegetables until tender, about 10 minutes. Add remaining ingredients except apples. Reduce heat to medium-low; cover and simmer for 45 minutes. Add apples and simmer for an additional 40 minutes, or until apples are tender and rice is cooked.

Right next to jumping into a pile of leaves, kids like nothing
more than bobbing for apples! An easy recipe for fun...
fill a galvanized tub with water, toss in a dozen or so apples;
add kids. The secret? Grabbing the apple stem in your teeth.

Butternut Squash & Apple Soup   *Makes 4 servings*

2 slices bacon
1/2 c. onions, chopped
1 c. leeks, chopped
1 clove garlic, minced
1/2 bay leaf
salt and pepper to taste
2-1/2 c. chicken broth
1 Granny Smith apple, peeled,
    cored and chopped

1-1/4 lbs. butternut squash,
    peeled, seeded and cut into
    1-inch cubes
hot water as needed
2 T. sour cream
Garnish: additional sour cream,
    chopped apples

Cook bacon in a large saucepan over medium heat until crisp. Remove
bacon, crumble and set aside. Add onions, leeks, garlic, bay leaf, salt and
pepper to drippings in pan; stir and sauté until soft. Add broth, apple and
squash; simmer for 15 minutes, or until squash is tender. Discard bay
leaf. Working in batches, carefully purée mixture in a blender; return to
pan. Add hot water to thin as desired; stir in sour cream. Heat just until
warmed through. Spoon into bowls; sprinkle with reserved bacon.
Garnish with a dollop of sour cream and a spoonful of chopped apples.

A centerpiece in a snap! Nestle a plump candle in the center
of a simple glass salad or punch bowl, then fill around
it with small apples.

Cider Pork Stew

Makes 6 to 8 servings

2 to 2-1/2 lbs. pork shoulder roast, cubed and fat trimmed
Optional: 1 T. oil
3 potatoes, peeled and cut into 1/2-inch cubes
3 carrots, peeled and cut into 1/2-inch slices
2 onions, sliced
1/2 c. celery, coarsely chopped
2/3 c. apple, peeled, cored and coarsely chopped
2 c. apple cider or apple juice
3 T. quick-cooking tapioca, uncooked
1 t. caraway seed
1 t. salt
1/4 t. pepper
Optional: snipped fresh chives

If desired, brown pork in oil in a large skillet over medium heat. Place pork in a 5-quart slow cooker. Add vegetables and apple; set aside. In a bowl, combine remaining ingredients except optional chives. Pour over pork mixture in slow cooker. Cover and cook on low setting for 10 to 12 hours, or on high setting for 5 to 6 hours, until pork is tender. If desired, top each serving with a sprinkle of snipped chives.

Soup suppers are a fuss-free way to get together with
friends, neighbors and family. Each family brings a
favorite soup to share, along with the recipe.
What a delicious way to try a variety of soups!

Mulligatawny Soup

Makes 6 to 7 servings

2 boneless, skinless chicken
   breasts
1 apple, cored and cubed
4 T. butter, sliced
1 c. onion, chopped
1 c. celery, chopped
1 c. carrots, peeled and diced
1 t. sugar
2 T. curry powder

1/2 t. ground mace
1/2 to 1 t. ground ginger
1 t. salt
1/2 t. pepper
14-1/2 oz. can crushed or diced
   tomatoes
8-oz. can tomato sauce
1 to 2 T. lemon juice

Cover chicken with water in a large saucepan. Cook over medium heat until chicken is tender, about 40 minutes. Set aside chicken to cool and dice; reserve broth in pan. Meanwhile, in a skillet over medium heat, sauté apple in butter. Add onion, celery, carrots, sugar, seasonings and enough water to cover vegetables. Simmer until vegetables are tender but not mushy. Add reserved chicken broth, tomatoes with juice and tomato sauce. Simmer over low heat for 40 minutes, stirring occasionally. Shortly before serving time, stir in chicken and lemon juice.

Whenever we bite into a juicy apple, we have Johnny Appleseed to thank. History tells us he traveled westward planting seeds he had collected from cider presses in Pennsylvania. Why not celebrate his birthday on September 26th? A fun and tasty history lesson for the kids!

Pumpkin-Apple Soup

2 T. butter
1 onion, diced
2 green apples, peeled, cored
    and diced
1 T. all-purpose flour
4 c. chicken broth
3 c. canned pumpkin
2 T. brown sugar, packed

1 t. cinnamon
1 t. nutmeg
1 t. ground ginger
1 c. apple juice
1/2 c. half-and-half
salt and pepper to taste
Garnish: toasted pumpkin seeds

Melt butter in a saucepan over medium heat. Add onion and apples; sauté until soft. Stir in flour; cook and stir for 2 to 3 minutes. Gradually whisk in broth; stir in pumpkin, sugar and spices. Bring to a boil; reduce heat to medium-low. Simmer, covered, for 25 minutes. Working in batches, carefully transfer to a blender; purée until smooth. Return to pan; add apple juice, half-and-half, salt and pepper. Heat until warmed through. Sprinkle individual bowls with pumpkin seeds.

Chances are there's a list of bike paths in your area. Gather the family together and enjoy the fall colors on a tree-lined path. Pack a thermos of icy cider to enjoy along the way.

Spicy Cabbage-Apple Slaw

2 c. shredded green and red
    cabbage mix
2 c. Red Delicious apples, cored
    and chopped
1/2 c. celery, chopped
2 T. chopped walnuts, toasted

2 T. golden raisins
1/2 c. plain yogurt
2 T. apple juice
1 T. honey
1/2 t. cinnamon

In a large serving bowl, combine cabbage mix, apples, celery, walnuts
and raisins; toss well. Combine remaining ingredients in a small bowl,
stirring well. Pour yogurt mixture over cabbage mixture; toss well. Cover
and chill for at least 30 minutes before serving.

Molded gelatin salads were everywhere in the 1950s, and they're still a refreshing make-ahead dish. Vintage copper molds can often be found at flea markets... dress up a kitchen wall with a whimsical display.

Winter Fruit Salad

2 oranges, peeled and sectioned
1 grapefruit, peeled and sectioned
2 apples, peeled, cored and diced
2 pears, peeled, cored and diced
2 bananas, sliced

1 c. red seedless grapes
1 c. apple cider
1 T. lemon juice
1-1/2 c. mayonnaise
6 leaves lettuce

Mix together all fruits; stir in cider and lemon juice. Chill for 2 to 3 hours. Drain, reserving juice. Combine mayonnaise and 1/3 cup reserved fruit juice. Arrange salad on lettuce leaves; drizzle with mayonnaise mixture.

If you bought a bunch of fresh herbs for a recipe that calls for just a couple of tablespoons, chop the extra herbs and add to a tossed salad. Fresh parsley, mint, dill, chives and basil all add zest.

Grilled Chicken Salad with Apple Dressing

Serves 4

4 boneless, skinless chicken
    breasts
salt and pepper to taste
1 c. apple, peeled and chopped
1/2 c. apple juice
1 T. cider vinegar

1 t. cornstarch
16-oz. pkg. mixed salad greens
1/4 c. sliced almonds, toasted
1/2 c. shredded Cheddar cheese
1/2 c. red pepper, sliced
3/4 c. crumbled blue cheese

Season chicken with salt and pepper. Grill on a lightly greased grill over medium-high heat until juices run clear when pierced. Cool; slice or cube chicken. Meanwhile, combine apple juice, apple, vinegar and cornstarch. Cook and stir over medium heat until thickened. Cool in refrigerator. To serve, divide salad greens among 4 salad plates. On each plate, arrange almonds, Cheddar cheese, red pepper, blue cheese and chicken. Drizzle with dressing; serve immediately.

Shake up a simple vinaigrette dressing. Combine 2 tablespoons cider vinegar, 6 tablespoons olive oil and one teaspoon Dijon mustard in a small jar, twist on the lid and shake well.
Add salt and pepper to taste.

Grandma's Waldorf Salad

Serves 6

2 Gala apples, cored and diced
1 Granny Smith apple, cored
   and diced
1/2 c. chopped pecans or walnuts

1/2 c. celery, diced
1/3 c. sweetened dried cranberries
1/3 c. mayonnaise

Stir together all ingredients in a large bowl. Cover and chill until serving time.

For a fun after-school snack that's ready in a jiffy,
stuff a hollowed-out apple with peanut butter and raisins.

Crunchy Apple-Pear Salad

Serves 6

2 apples, cored and cubed
2 pears, cored and thinly sliced
1 T. lemon juice
2 heads butter lettuce, torn into
    bite-size pieces
1/2 c. crumbled gorgonzola
    cheese

1 c. oil
6 T. cider vinegar
1/2 c. sugar
1 t. celery seed
1/2 t. salt
1/4 t. pepper
1/2 c. chopped walnuts, toasted

Toss apples and pears with lemon juice; drain. Arrange lettuce on 6 salad
plates; top with apples, pears and cheese. Combine remaining ingredients
except walnuts in a jar with a tight-fitting lid. Cover; shake well until
dressing is blended and sugar dissolves. Drizzle salad with dressing;
sprinkle with walnuts. Serve immediately.

Carrying a salad to a school potluck or a family picnic?
Mix it up in a plastic zipping bag instead of a bowl,
seal and set it on ice in a picnic cooler. No more
worries about leaks or spills!

Gingered Chicken & Fruit Salad   *Makes 8 servings*

1-1/2 to 2 c. mayonnaise
2 T. ground ginger
2 c. cooked chicken breast, cubed
1 c. green and/or red seedless
     grapes, halved lengthwise
3 Red Delicious apples, peeled,
     cored and diced

3 Granny Smith apples, peeled,
     cored and diced
1 c. pineapple chunks
1/2 c. slivered almonds

In a small bowl, stir together mayonnaise and ginger; set aside. Combine remaining ingredients in a large bowl. Add mayonnaise mixture; toss lightly until well blended and coated. Cover and chill until serving time.

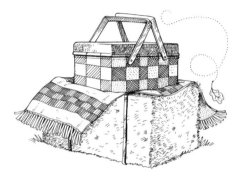

Plan a trip to the local apple orchard for a fall outing...
swirling leaves and the sweet smell of apples make it the
ideal picnic spot! Toss a couple sawhorses and length of
plywood in the back of a truck for a fast picnic table
and borrow a few straw bales for seating.

Apple Orchard Salad

Makes 6 to 8 servings

2 apples, peeled, cored and diced
1/2 c. golden raisins or sweetened
    dried cranberries
2 stalks celery, sliced

1/2 c. chopped walnuts
1/4 c. mayonnaise
2 T. orange juice

Combine all ingredients except mayonnaise and orange juice in a serving bowl; toss to mix well. In a small bowl, blend mayonnaise and juice; mix well and toss with fruit mixture. Cover and chill until serving time.

Turn apples into mini candle holders...just hollow out,
slip a votive inside and float along with some colorful
leaves in an old-fashioned copper wash tub.

Chilled Apple & Cheese Salad

Makes 6 servings

3-oz. pkg. lemon gelatin mix
1 c. boiling water
3/4 c. cold water
2/3 c. red apple, cored and
    finely chopped

1/4 c. celery, chopped
1/3 c. shredded Cheddar cheese

In a bowl, dissolve gelatin in boiling water. Stir in cold water; chill until partially set. Fold in remaining ingredients. Pour into a 3-cup mold. Cover and chill 3 hours, or until firm. Unmold onto a serving plate.

An easy way to core apples and peaches...slice fruit
in half and then use a melon baller to scoop out the core.

Prosciutto, Brie & Apple Panini   *Makes 2 sandwiches*

1/4 c. butter, softened
1 green onion, finely chopped
1/2 t. lemon juice
1/4 t. Dijon mustard
4 slices sourdough bread
3/4 lb. prosciutto or deli ham,
    thinly sliced

8-oz. round brie cheese, cut into
    4 pieces and rind removed
1 Granny Smith apple, peeled,
    cored and thinly sliced

In a bowl, beat butter until creamy. Stir in onion, lemon juice and mustard until smooth. Spread half the butter mixture on one side of 2 bread slices; place butter-side down on a heated panini maker or griddle. Top with prosciutto or ham, cheese and apple slices. Top with remaining bread slices; spread remaining butter mixture on the outside. Cook until toasted on both sides and cheese is melted.

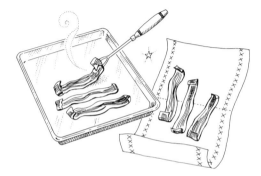

Enjoy all the scrumptious flavor of bacon with none of the mess! Arrange bacon slices on a baking sheet. Bake at 350 degrees for 15 to 20 minutes, until it's as crisp as you like. Drain well on paper towels.

Peanut Butter Apple-Bacon Sandwich

Makes 4 sandwiches

8 slices applewood smoked bacon
8 slices whole-grain bread
1/4 c. peach preserves
1 to 2 apples, cored and thinly
    sliced

1/4 c. creamy peanut butter
2 to 3 T. butter, softened and
    divided

In a skillet over medium heat, cook bacon until crisp; drain bacon on paper towels. Spread 4 slices of bread with preserves; layer apple and bacon slices over preserves. Spread remaining bread slices with peanut butter; close sandwiches. Spread tops of sandwiches with half of butter. Place sandwiches butter-side down on a griddle over medium heat. Spread remaining butter on unbuttered side of sandwiches. Cook 2 to 3 minutes per side, until bread is toasted and sandwiches are heated through. Serve warm.

Whip up this super-simple veggie dip! Blend one cup cottage cheese, 1/4 cup plain Greek yogurt, one tablespoon minced onion, one teaspoon dried parsley and 1/4 teaspoon dill weed. Serve with bite-size fresh vegetables...a great go-with for sandwich suppers.

Apricot-Cashew Salad Sandwiches

Makes 4 sandwiches

2 c. cooked turkey, diced
1 Granny Smith apple, peeled,
    cored and diced
1 c. celery, chopped
1/4 c. chopped cashews
1/4 c. dried apricots, finely
    chopped
1/2 c. mayonnaise

1/4 c. sour cream
2 T. apricot preserves
1/4 t. ground ginger
1/8 t. nutmeg
1/8 t. pepper
8 slices sandwich bread
4 lettuce leaves

Toss together turkey, apple, celery, cashews and apricots in a large bowl; set aside. Whisk together mayonnaise, sour cream, preserves and spices in a separate bowl; spoon over turkey mixture and fold in until well blended. Spoon mixture evenly onto 4 slices of bread. Top with lettuce leaf and remaining bread slices.

If your silverware needs polishing before the holidays, try this
quick & easy method for sparkling results. Line a baking pan
with aluminum foil, arrange silverware over foil and sprinkle
with baking soda to coat. Cover with boiling water and
let soak until the tarnish is magically gone!

Ham Steak & Apples Skillet

Makes 6 servings

3 T. butter
1/2 c. brown sugar, packed
1 T. Dijon mustard

2 c. apples, cored and diced
2 1-lb. bone-in ham steaks

Melt butter in a large skillet over medium heat. Add brown sugar and mustard; bring to a simmer. Add apples; cover and simmer for 5 minutes. Top apples with ham steaks. Cover with a lid; simmer for about 10 minutes more, until apples are tender. Remove ham to a platter and cut into serving-size pieces. Top ham with apples and sauce.

Sew a blanket stitch around the edges of a vintage
tea towel to make a basket liner...what a pretty way
to keep rolls warm throughout dinner!

Autumn Apple-Cheddar Chicken   *Makes 6 servings*

5 to 6 boneless, skinless chicken
   breasts
2 sleeves round buttery crackers,
   crushed
1/2 c. plus 3 T. butter, melted
1/4 c. all-purpose flour

3/4 c. milk
10-3/4 oz. can Cheddar cheese
   soup
1 c. shredded Cheddar cheese
3 Golden Delicious apples, cored
   and sliced

Place chicken in a large pot of boiling water. Cook for 8 to 10 minutes; arrange chicken in a greased 13"x9" baking pan and set aside. Combine crumbs with 1/2 cup butter; mix thoroughly and set aside. Add remaining butter to a saucepan; stir in flour and cook about one minute, stirring often. Add milk, soup and cheese; stir to blend until cheese is melted. Cover chicken with cheese sauce; top with sliced apples and sprinkle with cracker mixture. Bake, covered, at 350 degrees for 35 to 40 minutes.

All-day slow cooking works wonders on inexpensive, less-tender cuts of beef. Chuck roast, round steak and stew beef cook up juicy and delicious.

Apple Butter BBQ Spareribs   *Makes 4 to 6 servings*

4 lbs. pork spareribs, cut into
    serving-size pieces
salt and pepper to taste

16-oz. jar apple butter
18-oz. bottle barbecue sauce
1 onion, quartered

Sprinkle ribs with salt and pepper. Place ribs on rimmed baking sheets. Bake at 350 degrees for 30 minutes; drain. Meanwhile, blend together apple butter and barbecue sauce in a bowl; set aside. Transfer ribs to a slow cooker. Top with onion; drizzle sauce mixture over all. Cover and cook on low setting for 7 to 8 hours.

For the best pie apples, you can always count on
Jonathan, Winesap, Braeburn, Fuji, Rome Beauty,
Granny Smith and Pippin apples.

Sausage & Apple Skillet

Makes 2 servings

3 T. butter, divided
14-oz. pkg. smoked pork
    sausage, sliced
1 Granny Smith apple, peeled,
    cored and sliced

1 onion, sliced
1 c. apple cider
2 T. fresh sage, chopped
2 T. lemon juice
salt and pepper to taste

Melt one tablespoon butter in a skillet over medium heat; add sausage. Cook until beginning to brown, about 5 minutes, turning occasionally. Remove sausage from skillet and set aside. Add apple and onion to skillet; sauté until tender and golden, about 5 minutes, stirring often. Add cider and sage; increase heat to high. Cook and stir for about 2 minutes; stir in lemon juice, salt and pepper. With a slotted spoon, transfer apple mixture to 2 plates; top with sausage. Whisk remaining butter into juices in skillet; drizzle over sausage.

If you're cooking rice for dinner, why not make some extra?
Frozen in one-cup serving containers, it's easy to reheat
later in the week for a quick lunch or dinner. Especially handy
if you prefer brown rice, which can take a lot longer
to cook than white rice.

Chicken Bombay

Makes 4 servings

1/4 c. butter, melted
1 T. curry powder
1 tart apple, peeled, cored
and chopped

1 onion, chopped
3 lbs. chicken, cut up
2 c. cooked rice

Spread butter in a 13"x9" baking pan; add curry powder and mix well.
Stir in apple and onion. Bake, uncovered, at 400 degrees for 5 minutes.
Add chicken to pan, skin-side down. Cover and bake for 25 minutes.
Turn chicken over and bake, uncovered, an additional 25 minutes, or
until chicken juices run clear. Remove chicken to a serving platter; stir
cooked rice into pan juices and serve.

Add a zesty marinade to plastic zipping bags of uncooked
chicken and freeze. The chicken will be deliciously
seasoned when you thaw it for cooking.

Apple-Glazed Pork Roast

Serves 8 to 10

4-lb. pork loin roast
salt and pepper to taste
6 apples, cored and quartered

1/4 c. apple juice
3 T. brown sugar, packed
1 t. ground ginger

Season roast on all sides with salt and pepper. Place roast on a baking sheet and brown on both sides under a broiler. Arrange apples in a slow cooker; top with roast. In a bowl, whisk together juice, brown sugar and ginger; drizzle over roast. Cover and cook on high setting for 6 hours, or until roast is no longer pink in the center and apples are tender.

A cast-iron skillet is wonderful for cooking up homestyle dinners. If it hasn't been used in awhile, season it first. Rub it lightly with oil, bake at 300 degrees for an hour and let it cool completely in the oven. Now it's ready for many more years of good cooking!

Bacon & Apple Pork Chops

Serves 6

6 boneless pork chops
garlic powder, salt and pepper
    to taste
2 T. olive oil
3 thick-cut slices bacon, diced

1/2 c. onion, diced
1 to 2 cloves garlic, minced
2 apples, peeled, cored and diced
Garnish: honey

Sprinkle pork chops on both sides with seasonings; set aside. Heat oil in a cast-iron skillet over medium-high heat. Add chops; cook just until browned on both sides. Reduce heat to medium-low. Cover and cook until chops are no longer pink in the center; do not overcook. Meanwhile, in a separate skillet over medium heat, cook bacon until crisp. Push bacon to one side of the skillet. Add onion and garlic to the other side; cook until onion starts to soften. Add apples; stir contents of skillet together. Simmer for about 10 minutes, until apples are soft, reducing heat if necessary. To serve, spoon apple mixture over chops; drizzle with a small amount of honey.

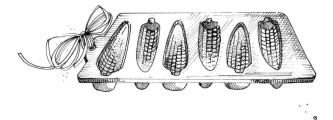

Just for fun, bake your next batch of cornbread in an old-fashioned corn stick pan...the kind that makes cornbread sticks shaped like ears of corn. Kids will love 'em!

Apple-Spice Country Ribs

Serves 4 to 6

2 to 3 lbs. boneless country
    pork ribs
3 baking apples, cored and
    cut into wedges
1 onion, thinly sliced
2/3 c. apple cider

1 t. cinnamon
1 t. allspice
1/2 t. salt
1/4 t. pepper
mashed potatoes or
    cooked rice

Place all ingredients except potatoes in a 5-quart slow cooker; stir to coat. Cover and cook on low setting for 7 to 9 hours. Juices will thicken as they cool; stir if separated. Serve ribs and sauce from slow cooker with mashed potatoes or hot cooked rice. (If bone-in ribs are used, slice into serving-size portions.)

Hand out plastic zipping bags filled with crayons, mini coloring books and stickers to little ones. They'll be happy creating crayon masterpieces while waiting for dinner or an activity to begin.

Apple-Stuffed Turkey Breast

Serves 10

1-1/2 c. long grain & wild rice,
    uncooked
2 apples, peeled, cored
    and chopped
1 onion, finely chopped

1/2 c. sweetened dried cranberries
3 c. water
4 to 5-lb. boneless, skinless
    turkey breast

Combine rice, apples, onion and cranberries in a slow cooker; pour water over top. Mix well. Place turkey on top of rice mixture. Cover and cook on low setting for 8 to 9 hours, until turkey juices run clear when pierced.

As soon as a casserole dish is empty, pop it into a sink
full of hot, soapy water to speed clean-up...
saves oodles of scrubbing time!

New England Wild Rice & Apples

Serves 4

2 T. onion, minced
1/2 c. butter, melted and divided
2 4-oz. pkgs. wild rice, cooked
1 Granny Smith apple, peeled,
    cored and chopped
1 McIntosh apple, cored
    and chopped

1 c. bread crumbs
1/2 c. chopped walnuts
1/4 c. orange juice
zest of one orange, chopped

In a skillet over medium heat, lightly sauté onion in 3 tablespoons butter. Combine onion and remaining butter with remaining ingredients. Mix well; transfer to a greased 2-quart casserole dish. Cover and bake at 325 degrees for 35 minutes, until apples are tender.

Taking a dish to share? Table tents let everyone know
what goodies await in potluck dishes! Fold an index in half
and jot down or rubber stamp the recipe name on
the front...be sure to add the cook's name.

Brown Sugar Applesauce

Makes 6 to 8 servings

3 lbs. cooking apples, peeled,
    cored and sliced
1/2 c. brown sugar, packed

1 t. cinnamon
1-1/2 T. lemon juice
Garnish: cinnamon

Combine all ingredients in a slow cooker. Cover and cook on high setting
for 3 hours, stirring occasionally. Mash with a potato masher to desired
consistency. Sprinkle portions with cinnamon.

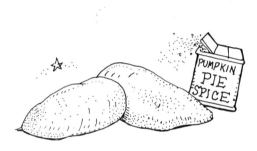

Serving sweet potatoes? Add a dash of
pumpkin pie spice...delicious!

Scalloped Sweet Potatoes & Apples   *Makes 6 servings*

2 sweet potatoes, boiled, peeled
    and sliced
2 tart apples, peeled, cored
    and sliced

1/2 c. brown sugar, packed
1 t. salt
1/4 c. butter, sliced

Layer half the potatoes in a buttered 13"x9" baking pan. Layer half the
apple slices. Sprinkle with half the sugar and salt; dot with half the butter.
Repeat with remaining ingredients. Bake, uncovered, at 350 degrees for
one hour.

Have fun apple picking with your children! To help little ones reach up into the trees, cut a 2-liter soda bottle in half around the middle. Tuck a broomstick into the spout and tape together. Just tap an apple gently and it should drop right into the bottle scoop.

Noodle Pudding with Apples

Makes 10 to 12 servings

16-oz. pkg. medium egg noodles, cooked
2 apples, peeled, cored and grated
1 c. chopped walnuts
1/2 c. golden raisins
juice of one lemon
1/2 to 1 c. butter, melted
1 c. sugar
4 eggs, beaten
1 c. orange juice

Gently toss cooked noodles, apples, walnuts and raisins together in a large bowl; set aside. Combine remaining ingredients in another bowl; stir into noodle mixture. Spread in a buttered 13"x9" baking pan. Bake, uncovered, at 350 degrees for 40 minutes, or until hot and bubbly.

The most indispensible ingredient of all good home cooking...
love, for those you are cooking for.

– Sophia Loren

Grandma's Holiday Stuffing

Serves 8 to 10

1 large loaf day-old bread, torn
Optional: day-old corn muffins,
 broken up
1/2 c. butter
1 onion, diced
3 stalks celery, diced
Optional: 1/2 c. sliced mushrooms

2 tart apples, cored and diced
1/2 c. walnuts, coarsely chopped
1/2 c. raisins
1/2 to 3/4 c. water
1/2 to 1 T. poultry seasoning
dried parsley to taste
salt and pepper to taste

Spread torn bread in a large baking pan; mix in muffins, if using. Bake, uncovered, at 250 degrees for about 30 minutes, until dried out. Set aside to cool. Meanwhile, melt butter over low heat in a large skillet; sauté onion, celery and mushrooms, if using, until tender. Add apples, walnuts and raisins; stir to coat with butter. Mix in water and seasonings; pour over bread and toss to moisten. Add a little more water if bread is very dry. Use to stuff a 12 to 15-pound turkey before roasting; do not overstuff. Or spread stuffing in a lightly greased 9"x5" loaf pan and bake at 350 degrees for 30 to 40 minutes.

A hot cup of flavored coffee is oh-so welcome after a hearty meal. Simply add a few drops of almond or cinnamon extract to the ground coffee in the percolator basket before brewing.

Braised Cabbage & Apples

Serves 6

3 slices bacon
1 yellow onion, peeled and
    thinly sliced
1 head cabbage, shredded
1/2 c. cider vinegar
1/2 c. apple cider

1/2 c. sugar
4 whole cloves
2 tart apples, peeled, cored
    and thinly sliced
salt and pepper to taste

Cook bacon in a large, deep skillet over medium heat until crisp. Drain bacon on paper towels, reserving drippings in skillet. Crumble bacon and set aside. Sauté onion in reserved drippings over medium heat until tender and golden. In a bowl, toss cabbage with vinegar; add to skillet along with remaining ingredients except salt and pepper. Simmer, uncovered, over low heat until cabbage is tender, about 20 minutes. Discard cloves. Season to taste with salt and pepper; serve garnished with crumbled bacon.

A mini dried-apple wreath makes a fragrant,
fall napkin ring...ready in seconds!

Honey-Baked Apples & Pears

Serves 4

2 apples, peeled, cored and each
    sliced into 8 wedges
1 pear, peeled, cored and sliced
    into 8 wedges

2/3 c. honey
2 T. water
1-1/2 t. cinnamon
3 T. butter, sliced

Arrange apples and pears in a greased one-quart casserole dish; set aside. Combine honey, water and cinnamon; pour over apple mixture. Dot with butter. Bake, uncovered, at 350 degrees for 25 minutes, or until fruit is tender.

Top off jar lids of homemade butters with a vintage hankie, then tie on a sweetly printed ribbon.

Pumpkin-Apple Butter

Makes 5 cups

2 15-oz. cans pumpkin
2 c. applesauce
2/3 c. brown sugar, packed
1 t. cinnamon

1 t. nutmeg
1-1/2 T. fresh ginger, peeled
   and grated

In a saucepan over medium heat, stir together all ingredients until blended. Bring to a boil, stirring constantly. Reduce heat to low. Simmer, uncovered, stirring often for 30 minutes, or until mixture is very thick. Cool; spoon into sterilized containers and add lids. Keep refrigerated for up to 2 weeks.

An apple a day keeps the doctor away.

–Old Saying

Apple-Ginger Chutney

Makes 6 jars

4 Granny Smith apples, peeled,
 cored and chopped
2 c. onion, minced
1 red pepper, minced
1/4 c. fresh ginger, peeled
 and minced
1 c. golden raisins
1-1/2 c. cider vinegar

1-1/2 c. dark brown sugar,
 packed
3/4 t. dry mustard
3/4 t. salt
1/2 t. red pepper flakes
6 1/2-pint canning jars and
 lids, sterilized

Combine all ingredients in a large saucepan over medium-high heat.
Bring to a boil, stirring frequently. Reduce heat to low. Simmer for
40 minutes, stirring occasionally, until thickened. Spoon chutney into
sterilized jars; cool slightly and add lids. Keep refrigerated up to 2 weeks.

Cut a pan of bar cookies into circles using a round
cookie cutter. Arrange cookies in a glass tumbler,
separated by circles of wax paper. Tie a circle of
fabric with jute over the tumbler's top...clever!

Ashley's Apple Butter Bars

Makes about 2-1/2 dozen

1-1/2 c. all-purpose flour
1 t. baking soda
1 t. salt
1-1/2 c. quick-cooking oats,
    uncooked

1-1/2 c. sugar
1 c. butter, melted
1-1/2 c. apple butter
1 c. chopped pecans or walnuts

Combine flour, baking soda and salt in a large bowl. Stir in oats and sugar. Add melted butter; mix well until crumbly. Press half of mixture into a greased 13"x9" baking pan; set aside. In a separate bowl, mix apple butter and nuts together: spread over crumb mixture. Sprinkle with remaining crumb mixture. Bake at 350 degrees for 50 to 60 minutes, until golden. Cool completely; slice into bars.

Make short work of chopping nuts...seal them
in a plastic zipping bag and roll with a rolling pin.
No muss, no fuss!

Diana's Apple Crisp Cookies

Makes about 7 dozen

1-1/2 c. margarine, softened
1-1/2 c. dark brown sugar,
    packed
1 c. sugar
0.7-oz. pkg. spiced apple
    drink mix
1 T. cinnamon
1-1/2 t. baking powder
1-1/2 t. baking soda

1/2 t. salt
3 eggs, beaten
2 t. vanilla extract
3 c. all-purpose flour
3 c. long-cooking oats, uncooked
1-1/2 c. raisins
1-1/2 c. dried apples, chopped
1 c. chopped walnuts

In a very large bowl, combine margarine, sugars, drink mix, cinnamon, baking powder, baking soda and salt. Mix well; blend in eggs and vanilla. Blend in as much of the flour as possible; stir in remaining ingredients. Drop dough by rounded teaspoonfuls onto ungreased baking sheets. Bake at 350 degrees for 10 to 12 minutes, until light golden. Cool on wire racks.

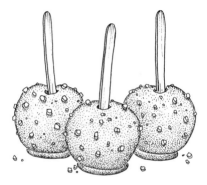

After coating apples in caramel or candy mixture,
quickly dip them into chopped nuts or sprinkles
for an extra-special treat.

Shiny Red Candy Apples

Makes 10 apples

4 c. sugar
1 c. butter
1/4 c. white vinegar
1/4 c. boiling water
1/2 t. red food coloring

1/4 c. red cinnamon candies
10 lollipop sticks or
   wooden skewers
10 Granny Smith apples

Combine sugar, butter, vinegar, boiling water and food coloring in a large heavy metal saucepan. Cook over low heat until sugar dissolves. Increase heat to medium-high; boil without stirring for about 10 minutes, until mixture reaches the hard-crack stage, or 290 to 310 degrees on a candy thermometer. Remove from heat; stir in cinnamon candies and let stand until bubbles subside. Insert sticks into apples. Dip apples into mixture; swirl to coat and dip into ice water to harden candy coating. Place on a lightly buttered baking pan until set. Store in a cool, dry place.

It's easy to save extra whipped cream! Dollop heaping tablespoonfuls onto a chilled baking sheet and freeze. Remove from the baking sheet and store in a plastic zipping bag. To use, place dollops on dessert servings and let stand a few minutes.

Spicy Apple Dump Cake

Makes 8 servings

4 to 5 Fuji or Gala apples, peeled,
  cored and thinly sliced
1-1/4 c. apple juice, divided
18-1/4 oz. pkg. spice cake mix

1/2 c. butter, melted
1/4 c. brown sugar, packed
1/4 c. rolled oats, uncooked
1/4 c. pecans, coarsely chopped

Arrange apple slices in the bottom of a lightly greased 13"x9" baking
pan. Pour 1/2 cup apple juice over apples. Sprinkle dry cake mix over
apples and smooth it evenly across the pan. Sprinkle remaining apple
juice evenly across cake mix layer; drizzle with butter. For topping, mix
brown sugar, oats and pecans with a fork until no lumps remain. Sprinkle
evenly over top. Bake at 350 degrees for about 40 minutes, until cake
begins to turn golden.

Scoops of ice cream are a perfect garnish for warm pies and puddings. Serve them in a snap...simply scoop ahead of time into paper muffin cup liners and freeze on a baking sheet.

French Apple Crisp

Makes 12 servings

1/4 c. butter, divided
4 c. apples, peeled, cored
   and sliced
1/4 c. unsweetened apple juice
2/3 c. sugar, divided

1/8 t. cinnamon
1/2 c. blanched almonds,
   finely chopped
1/2 c. all-purpose flour
1/2 t. vanilla extract

Melt 2 tablespoons butter in a large skillet over medium heat. Sauté apples in butter until tender, about 5 minutes. Remove from heat; pour apple juice over apples. Stir in 1/3 cup sugar and cinnamon. Let stand 30 minutes. Measure almonds, flour, and remaining sugar into a bowl. Cut in remaining butter with pastry blender or 2 knives until mixture resembles coarse meal. Add vanilla. Evenly spread apple mixture in a greased 2-quart casserole dish or individual ramekins. Sprinkle half of the flour mixture over the apples. Bake at 400 degrees for 15 minutes. Sprinkle remaining flour mixture on top. Bake an additional 15 minutes, or until golden. Serve warm.

'Tis the sweet, simple things of life
which are the real ones after all.

–Laura Ingalls Wilder

Apple Crunch Pie

Serves 6 to 8

2/3 c. sugar
1/4 c. all-purpose flour
1/2 t. nutmeg
1/2 t. cinnamon
1/8 t. salt

5 Granny Smith apples, peeled,
    cored and sliced
9-inch pie crust, unbaked
Optional 1/2 c. fresh cranberries
Garnish: cinnamon-sugar

Whisk sugar, flour, nutmeg, cinnamon and salt in a large bowl. Stir in apples and cranberries, if using; spoon into pie crust. Top with Crumb Topping; sprinkle with cinnamon-sugar. Bake at 425 degrees for 50 minutes, or until bubbly and crust is golden. Sprinkle with additional cinnamon-sugar.

Crumb Topping:

1 c. all-purpose flour
1/2 c. brown sugar, packed

1/4 c. butter, chilled

Mix ingredients together until crumbly.

Apple picking can be a fun family outing! The kids will be amazed to see all the different kinds of apples and so many are just the right size for little ones. Take a picnic and make a day of it, with fresh-picked apples for dessert!

Cran-Apple Cobbler

Makes 6 to 8 servings

1 T. butter, softened
2 Rome or Golden Delicious
    apples, peeled, cored and
    very thinly sliced
1/3 c. brown sugar, packed
3 T. all-purpose flour
1 t. cinnamon

14-oz. can whole-berry
    cranberry sauce
16-1/2 oz. tube refrigerated
    sugar cookie dough, sliced
    1/4-inch thick
Garnish: sugar

Coat the inside of a slow cooker with butter. Arrange apple slices in the
bottom; set aside. In a bowl, combine brown sugar, flour, cinnamon and
cranberry sauce; spoon over apples. Arrange cookie dough slices on top;
sprinkle with sugar. Cover and cook on low setting for 3 to 4 hours, until
bubbly and dough is set.

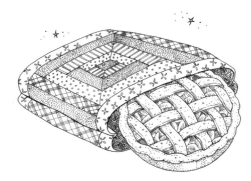

Taking a fresh-baked cobbler or pie to a family
get-together? Keep it warm in a cobbler cozy...simple
to make! Lay 2 placemats together, wrong-side out. Stitch
3 sides together, leaving one of the short ends open.
Turn right-side out...ready to tuck in your dessert!

Apple Brown Betty

Makes 6 to 8 servings

3 lbs. cooking apples, peeled,
    cored and cut into eighths
10 slices bread, cubed
1/2 t. cinnamon
1/4 t. nutmeg

1/8 t. salt
3/4 c. brown sugar, packed
1/2 c. butter, melted
Garnish: whipped topping

Place apples in a slow cooker. Combine remaining ingredients except topping; toss together and sprinkle over apples. Cover and cook on low setting 2 to 4 hours. Garnish with whipped topping.

INDEX

INDEX

Our Story

Back in 1984, we were next-door neighbors raising our families in the little town of Delaware, Ohio. Two moms with small children, we were looking for a way to do what we loved and stay home with the kids too. We had always shared a love of home cooking and making memories with family & friends and so, after many a conversation over the backyard fence, **Gooseberry Patch** was born.

We put together our first catalog at our kitchen tables, enlisting the help of our loved ones wherever we could. From that very first mailing, we found an immediate connection with many of our customers and it wasn't long before we began receiving letters, photos and recipes from these new friends. In 1992, we put together our very first cookbook, compiled from hundreds of these recipes and, the rest, as they say, is history.

Hard to believe it's been almost 40 years since those kitchen-table days! From that original little **Gooseberry Patch** family, we've grown to include an amazing group of creative folks who love cooking, decorating and creating as much as we do. Today, we're best known for our homestyle, family-friendly cookbooks, now recognized as national bestsellers.

One thing's for sure, we couldn't have done it without our friends all across the country. Each year, we're honored to turn thousands of your recipes into our collectible cookbooks. Our hope is that each book captures the stories and heart of all of you who have shared with us. Whether you've been with us since the beginning or are just discovering us, welcome to the **Gooseberry Patch** family!

Visit our website anytime
www.gooseberrypatch.com

Jo Ann & Vickie

1·800·854·6673